M000074671

On the Commerce of Thinking

JEAN-LUC NANCY

On the Commerce
of Thinking

Of Books and Bookstores

———————

Translated by David Wills

FORDHAM UNIVERSITY PRESS

NEW YORK 2009

This work was originally published in French as Jean-Luc
Nancy, *Sur le commerce des pensées: Du livre et de la librairie*
© 2005 Éditions Galilée, Paris.

This work has been published with the assistance of the
National Center for the Book—French Ministry of Culture.

Ouvrage publié avec le soutien du Centre national du
livre—ministère français chargé de la culture.

Fordham University Press has no responsibility for the
persistence or accuracy of URLs for external or third-party
Internet websites referred to in this publication and does
not guarantee that any content on such websites is, or will
remain, accurate or appropriate.

Library of Congress Cataloguing-in-Publication Data

Nancy, Jean-Luc
[Sur le commerce des pensées. English] On the commerce
of thinking : of books and bookstores / Jean-Luc Nancy ;
translated by David Wills.
    p. cm.   Includes bibliographical references.
ISBN 978-0-8232-3036-5 (alk. paper)— ISBN 978-0-8232-3037-2
(pbk.: alk. paper)
1. Booksellers and bookselling—Philosophy. 2. Books and
reading. I. Title.
Z278.N3613 2009   381'.4500201—dc22   2009003252

Printed in the United States of America

11 10 09   5 4 3 2 1   FIRST EDITION

*Commerce with books offers, for its part, the constancy
and ease of its service. It is at my side throughout my
course, and gives me succor wherever I am. It consoles
me in old age and solitude. It relieves me of the weight
of a tedious idleness, and extracts me at any time from
unpleasant company. It dulls the pangs of sorrow, unless
it be extreme and overpowering. In order to be distracted
from a troublesome imagination, one has only to take
refuge in books: they easily divert me toward themselves
and remove what is troubling me. Thus it is that they
by no means rebel when they see that I seek them out only
for lack of other more real, alive, and natural comforts;
they always receive me with the same countenance.*

MONTAIGNE, *Essays*, III, 3 ("Of Three Types of Commerce")

Bookstore, (Comm.): the bookstore, as a type of commerce, is worthy of consideration, provided that whoever undertakes it possesses the intelligence and enlightenment that it demands. This profession is to be regarded as one of the most noble and distinguished there is. Commerce in books is one of the oldest known trades; as long ago as the year of the world 1816 one witnessed a famous library built under the auspices of the third king of Egypt.

D'ALEMBERT AND DIDEROT, *Encyclopédie*

There appeared certain of those rare men who forever deserve mention in the history of printing and letters, those who, motivated by passion for art and full of the noble and courageous confidence that superior talents inspire in them—printers by profession, but people with a profound literary sensibility, capable of confronting every difficulty at once—developed the most daring projects.

DIDEROT, *"Historical and Political Letter Addressed to a Magistrate Concerning the Book Trade"*

CONTENTS

Translator's Foreword

Thinking Singular Plural

DAVID WILLS

The French title of Jean-Luc Nancy's book on books is *Sur le commerce des pensées*. I found myself obliged to render the plural *pensées*, with its echoes of Pascal and the rest (although perhaps not all the way to those small, delicate flowers we call "pansies"), as "thinking." Why, one might well wonder, would English be uncomfortable with a plural such as "thoughts" in the context of an essay on books and the bookstore? Why would that seem to imply an unacceptable crassness, or indeed commodification, of thinking, when that is precisely one of the things Nancy wants to evoke by means of the word *commerce*?

Answers to such questions would have to begin at the level of sonority—in French *pensée* (singular) is homonymic with *pensées* (plural)—and extend as far as the Germanic etymological network from which English *thinking* and *thought* emerge, in contrast to the Latinate *pensée*. Yet another line of resolution would have to investigate the different philologico-philosophical traditions of one or the other culture, a French tradition perhaps more at home with itself and with its pervasiveness, and so requiring less that *thought* be protected from the banalization or promiscuity of *thoughts*, an English one precisely nervous about such an assimilation of philosophical reflection to everyday cognitive processes.

Yet another, which brings me to my point, would have to raise the question of the book. First of all, obviously, such differences as that between the 18 × 21.5 cm. format and textured ivory laid paper ("watermarked with parallel lines from the wires on which the pulp was laid in the process of manufacture: opposed to *wove*"; Websters) of Nancy's Éditions Galilée text, and the 5.25 × 8 inch trim size of this volume, and by extension the different forms of bibliophilia that are practiced here or there and that give rise to all the different means by which the book is marketed, including, of course, online purchasing, and the success or failure of the bookstore—neighborhood or conglomerate—in preserving its niche as the preferred retail outlet for printed and bound texts.

But the logic of Nancy's discussion points to another relation between the Idea and its "delivery" in a book, namely, that when thinking or thought "reaches" the book it necessarily does so in a form that is the basis for commerce, and hence the importance of his plural. The book, and the bookstore, become the contexts within which quantities of thoughts get passed around, bought, sold, and exchanged: hence commodifiable, commercializable. But those thoughts, now irrevocably plural, are passed around not in some rarefied vacuum but among readers, also necessarily plural: among the members, therefore, of a community. If thoughts become the objects of commerce, it is precisely only because they imply and require such a community of readers.

The word *community* is never once used in Nancy's text, where the emphasis is less on readers than on reading. It is, however, common to much of his other writing, so much so that it amounts in his work to a grand philosophical project, asking simply, and complicatedly, what being together means in the wake of the monumental perversions and abortions of mass aspirations in the twentieth century. What community categorically does not mean, can no longer mean, is the sort of fusional melding of singularities that the previous century was witness to, not just because of how a mass came then to be misused, or to misuse itself but, more fundamentally, because the notion of singularity, subject, or individual presumed in numbers to comprise that mass is itself the most fraught of concepts: "What is a community? . . . The *common*, having-in-common or being-in-common, excludes from itself interior unity, subsistence, and presence in and by itself. Being with, being together, and even being 'united' are precisely not a matter of being 'one.'" In the book from which that quote is taken, and which inspires the title of this foreword, *Being Singular Plural*, published in France in 1996 in the shadow of a Sarajevo become the earth's "martyr-name," one of Nancy's vaunted words for a community beyond the violence of identitarian politics is *mêlée*. The word can mean everything from a wrestling match or rugby scrummage to a disorganized mélange or pell-mell free-for-all brawl. Nancy considers the risk of such uncontrolled intra- and interpersonal mixing, even to the point of forms of violence, to be far smaller than the risk of, and incontrovertibly documented facts of, violence stemming from social and political formations based on subjectivities and identities. What is required is to remake a culture and thinking that is not "crude or obscene like every thought of purity," for the simplistic praise of purity "has supported and still supports crimes."[1]

The commerce written of in *On the Commerce of Thinking* cannot, therefore, reduce to a mercantile exchange, even if that is an element within it. It is, rather, a commingling that has something of the *mêlée* about it (and indeed the word is used to describe the plurality of worlds that constitute reading), perhaps most evident in the originary contamination ("the *mêlée* is not accidental; it is originary"[2]) uncovered at the level of the signifier. If Nancy's reflection on books, thoughts, and their commerce seems to engender an inordinate attention to etymological nuance, it is because, in following the semantic traces, one finds not some touchstone of meaning but the very unstable mixing at work in the source, what gives rise to meaning as a movement of drift and divergence. Because a word, from the outset, determines its sense in comparison and contrast, in conversation and contact with other words, it begins as a pluralization that is an intercourse and a commerce. The verbal rough and tumble that makes for a book is therefore more than the fact of its being composed of more or less many words; it is similarly a function of each of those words being with itself as a plurality, being with itself as another to the point of being against itself.

Community is obviously not the predominant form of social or political being together that is in play in the case of the book, even if Nancy expresses a profound respect for the guild of professions that produce and sell books, and describes frequenting the bookstore as a profoundly sensual experience, savored even by those who are touched by words without reading them. Rather, the particular form of sharing relevant to the commerce of thinking, a thought's being with itself and being with others, is called "communication." And just as community contradicts the self-enclosed entities presumed to constitute it, breaking them open, making singularities plural, so communication is never a simple transmission but also, as Nancy writes below, "resonance, and dissemination—all the way to dispersion, metamorphosis, and reinterpretation." In being communicated thought disintegrates, becomes a book and hence the possibility of commerce.

📖

Sur le commerce des pensées is Nancy's main title. His subtitle is *Du livre et de la librairie*. If stylistic considerations led me to translate *pensées* into an English singular, a converse operation takes place in the subtitle, where it sounds better for us to hear *Of Books and Bookstores*, even if the French is in the singular. Logically speaking, that negates much of what I have just argued concerning *thought* vis-à-vis *thoughts*, especially as it and they relate to the book. Or rather, it sets up a countercurrent to what I have just argued, so that whatever truth there is in a mass/number distinction between English and French that can be traced from thinking to the book, a symmetrical persuasion runs back against that grain, raising like hackles the fibers of the page, from *books* to *thoughts*. I'd like to think that we have there a structural version of the oppositionality that, for Nancy, constitutes the book as double, as both open and closed, which makes *every single book books*, whatever language it is written in or translated into. For just as the unscrolling of the *volumen* came to be punctuated by the discontinuous pages of the codex format, so every discursive flow or unfurling is interrupted, ripped, even, by the eddies or undertow of other axes and networks of meaning, other words, other languages. As a result, thoughts regroup here as thinking whereas the book shatters there into books; from such quicksilver shards Jean-Luc Nancy has fashioned this one.

On the Commerce of Thinking

The first version of these pages was written in 2004 at the suggestion of the Quai des Brumes bookstore in Strasbourg. For the store's twentieth anniversary, the management wanted to make a gift of a book to its regular clients. At that point my text was entitled "Of Books and Bookstores," and it was published by the bookstore and Éditions La Fosse aux ours.

For this new version, Jean Le Gac has included sketches done at the time of a book-signing at the bookstore Le Passage in Alençon, among other drawings produced by him in the spirit of the illustrated book—in the sense that the illustration is neither a commentary on nor a visualization of the text, but something added to its savor, its scent, and its grain. [These illustrations from the Éditions Galilée publication have not been included in the English-language edition.]

This essay, therefore, in its desire to honor the commerce of books, is dedicated in the first place—thanks to chance—as much to the friendship of the Quai des brumes as to the welcome received from Le Passage. For this new version it is indebted to Éditions Galilée, which wishes to salute all those—booksellers, editors, printers, graphic designers, copyeditors—who make possible the commerce of books, that is to say, the sharing of an amorous and uninterrupted rewriting of the enigma.

On the Commerce of Thinking

Of Books and Bookstores

Liber: *membrane occurring between bark and wood,
between* cortex *and* lignum, *between exposed thought
and knotty intimacy, interface between outside and
inside, itself neither outside nor inside, turned toward
one as toward the other, turning one toward the other,
turning one back over into the other. Although the book
can become—digitized, immaterialized, and virtualized
as well as bound in leather and gilt-edged—however
slim it may become, it can be produced only by remaining
"for this reader pure block—transparent,"*[1] *through
which we gain access to nothing other than ourselves,
some to others but in each to hieroglyphics.*

The veritable property of the book, its *virtus opera-
tiva* or *vis magica*, or what we would have to call its
librarity, is to be found nowhere if not in the relation
it establishes and maintains between its opening and

closing. In contrast to the proverbial door, a book cannot be open or closed: it is always between the two, always passing from one state to the other.

Such a continuous and endlessly reversible transition—for the open book closes in exactly the same way that the closed book opens—derives from the fact that the book can be considered neither plainly as "container" nor quite simply as "content." It is not an object that can be put away on a shelf or placed on a table, but neither is it the printed text found on its pages. Instead, it shifts from one to the other, or else resides in the tension between the two. It produces that tension, provokes it, and doesn't stop maintaining it throughout its pages. But it also relaxes and appeases it, entrusting it to its volume as to a type of repository.

On the side of tension, expectation, and temptation, one finds the feverish intention from which the book always issues. No book ever flows from a source: one doesn't write a book as one writes a letter, memoir, or lampoon (*libelle*, "little book"). One projects, rather, an enterprise that thinks of itself, each time, as having no example and no imitator. One envisages delivering [*livrer*], or delivering oneself, as a thought that is perfect in itself and sufficient to itself, never a simple means of communication, representation, or imagination. A book is born in agitation and anxiety, in the fermentation of a form in search of itself, in search of a deployment and appeasement for its impatience.

On the side of repose, the book proposes its composition. The latter should not, all the same, be understood solely in the sense either of organization or construction, or, generally speaking, of the systematicity or indeed synesthesia that the unity of the book is presumed to imply and articulate. Rather, in a more modest and empirical manner, one must begin by recognizing the assemblage represented by its material oneness. Its binding and stitching create its volume: if it is "a book" in the transcendental or archetypal sense of the term, that is, if it responds to what is thought within the pure Idea of "book," that is another matter, which can be accounted for only by a reading.

It is already sufficient that pages succeed one

another and link one to another in the name of such an Idea. That supposes the linking not to be simply that of a logic or of a narration or exposition. Wherever one is in the business of presenting or indeed receiving a demonstration, history, description, or analysis, the form of oral discourse, that of the *lesson*—to give it its name—will suit just as well and even be preferable to the form of the book.

That is, moreover, the essential if not unique raison d'être, for those who teach: professors speak. Inasmuch as they are professors, they are speaking beings. If they write books, it is not in the same capacity. One could say the same thing, and in a strictly parallel manner, for painters, mechanics, lawyers, masons, doctors, etc. Each of those, as a member of a profession, professes, as it were, by means of gesture, word, or by one's conduct as a whole. But should one of them compose a book, and should that book be not just a "manual" of the knowledge professed, then we have another subject, another personage, indeed, another person, or other than a person, no less, one who becomes what is called the author of a book.

The term *manual* says it well: a manual contains—in a form and format that can be handled, *mani*pulated—a set of instructions relevant to the managing of a given theoretical or practical discipline. A manual is neither book nor teaching. No more than is what one calls a "treatise," which sets out the integrality of a body of knowledge or thinking. In the same way that the manual is designed for handling or maneuvering, the treatise is intended to permit the inspection and surveying of a domain, a geography or cosmogony of data or notions. Publications of that sort constitute *works*: they develop out of operational intentions and conduct, and open the way to other possible operations. Quite simply, they are means to ends located outside of themselves, in the world of theoretical or practical action. All works that militate, that are engaged in a cause, that carry demands—manifestoes, squibs, broadsheets, pamphlets, penny dreadfuls, pasquinades—also belong to this register.

The book is something else entirely. It doesn't constitute a means and, concomitantly, it would be difficult to place it within the category of ends.

For if it has no end outside of itself, neither is it in itself the end of any operation whatsoever.

That is not to say that one cannot, here and there, find in books—in certain books at the very least —elements of the manual or treatise, aspects of the encyclopedia or doctrinal collection, instructions for use or disciplinary insights, even precepts, advice, monitions, declarations or exhortations. In a symmetrical manner, neither can it be denied that the treatise, manual, or militant lampoon is capable of containing certain levels of expertise, or of echoing with certain emphases that would place those publications in the company of books. However, the essential question lies elsewhere: the book that must be our concern here cannot be identified as a distinct object or as a defined class of objects. It is far from being assimilable to the printed volume, even if it confers upon that volume certain of its most noteworthy values, including, in the very first place, the value of Idea *in itself* enfolded and *of itself* unravelable by means of which we truly identify a "book" when we use that word precisely in order to distinguish it from v*olume* and from *work*. Moreover, that is how the Latin word *liber* has traced its modern destiny, changing from "printed book" to simply "book," in its absolute sense, the absolute book if not the absolute as book.

The Idea and Character of the Book

If the Idea, in the acceptation that Plato conferred on the term, designates the veritable and intelligible Form—accomplished in its essence—of such and such a thing or reality (the Idea of man, of stone, of the lizard), then the Idea of the book could denote the delivery of an Idea. A book delivers [*un livre livre*]—it delivers, liberates, exposes, presents, manifests, reveals—a pure, essential and exclusive, inimitable, nonempirical form. If I say *The Divine Comedy* or *Lucien Leuwen*, *The Phenomenology of Spirit* or else *The Social Contract*, *A Season in Hell* or *Light in August*, I am pointing to such a form.

It is quite evident, in fact, that by uttering each of those titles—among millions of others—one does not in the first instance evoke the representation of a content of any sort (narrative, speculative, imaginative) but rather, well on this or the other side of the order of representations, the form of a contour, a sketch, a distinct and precise tracing, albeit not submitted to a determinate figuration, the suave Idea itself. The *title* of a book is precisely what carries this set of differential traits that comprise the form it is concerned with: neither figure, nor even drawing, face, or outline, but the demeanor or particular turn within which the idea is embodied: *The Beast in the Jungle* or *The Death of Virgil*.

For there must not be any separation here between "idea" and "body," no more than between an "ideality" and a "materiality." The ideality of the book is found in the body of its volume, in what keeps together pages whose succession and number (whatever that may be) in no way derive from an order of measure or quantity, but on the contrary from the diversified and articulated body of this unity of bearing that I have called "idea."

Perhaps it wouldn't be so bad to call this bearing and concrete ideality the *character* of the book: its distinctive mark, the specific, or better still, original imprint (if one is still allowed to use the word *original* today, and without wanting to reactivate some term evoking *genius*) of what has sometimes been called a "voice."

For the book to print the character of a voice, for

9

it to compose the type or typography of a vocal modulation, in short, of speech, brings it close, not unsurprisingly, to the oral reciting or teaching from which, a little earlier, we thought we could distinguish it.

Indeed, the professorial, professional, or professing spoken word is divided in two, by means of a dehiscence that lies deep within and barely visible. On the one hand, that speaking professes, and in those terms it is directed toward transmission, communication. However, on the other hand, it is able in itself to remain, as it were, extrinsic and foreign to such a transmission. That is what allowed Plato to make fun of those who repeat, the bards who recite poems, for failing to comprehend the content of their recitations. But on this point, as on so many others, Plato's anxiety is clear: he is in fact worried about himself, about knowing to what extent he himself understands properly the truth whose faithful recitation he undertakes to deliver.

Evidently the fact that Plato composed books is not unrelated to the circumstance that he was one of the very first among us to make books, whose character as written compositions he rarely failed to mark in a number of ways: he staged their writing and composition, as well as their reading by a slave charged with fetching the volume from the library.

Plato knew perfectly well that the Idea cannot do without its own delivery: it wishes to be exposed, unfolded, it must take on the bearing that behooves it, and for that must allow the turning, twists, contours, and detours of this bearing to be printed. The Idea requires its character.

Hence it is necessary, with an extraordinarily profound and pressing necessity, for the aspect of the spoken word that doesn't profess, the aspect that modulates and modalizes, that, in short, characterizes the aspect that *forms* the Idea—distinguished, if possible, from the aspect that informs concerning it—to declare itself and expose itself as a book.

Plato's book is a dialogue. One would commonly say that it *takes the form* of a dialogue, as though dialogue were one available form or genre among others. But in reality the dialogue or *dialogy* provides the essence of the book, or the Idea of its Idea. In essence the book speaks *to*, it is addressed, it addresses itself, it destines itself, it turns toward an interlocutor who is therefore a reader. The book doesn't speak *of*, it speaks *to*, or rather, it doesn't speak *of* without also speaking *to*, and in such a way that that address becomes indissociable, essentially undetachable from what is spoken or written "about."

The book is a dialogue: it confers upon the Idea the character of a dialogue. To that extent, its Idea does not preexist that character: it is itself the specific imprint of an address. Idea and Form denote here very precisely the form of address and, better yet, form *as* address.

A book is an address or an appeal. Beneath the melodic line of its singing there intones, without interruption, the continuous bass of its invitation, of its request, injunction, or prayer: "Read me! Read me!" (And that prayer murmurs still, even when the author declares "Don't read me!" or "Throw my book away!")

The Book's End in Itself

That is why, if the book is printed, the essence of its *impression* consists in the communication, resonance, and dissemination—all the way to dispersion, metamorphosis, and reinterpretation—of a voice, an irreducible orality: the difference of an intonation.

Why not, on that basis, think of the book as the Homeric corpus in its solely oral state, imprinted in the memory of bards and published by means of their peregrinations and recitations, each time anew? What there is of the *mythos* that subsists irreducibly, indeed irrepressibly, in the *logos*—presuming that there is no residue of sacred revelation—is precisely the tone of a recitation, the inflection of an address whereby, and by that means only, what is delivered is not in the first place sense but truth: the announcement of a possibility, of a chance for sense and for thinking.

It is significant that among the sacred books of the West the one that most lays claim to the title and appellation "book," namely, the Koran, claims an oral revelation: its written consignment only succeeds its recitation (which is the sense of the word *koran*), and the supposed perfection of language that is consigned thus is nothing other than that of the voice of dictation.

In fact, the idea of the book is indeed that of a perfection, of an accomplishment in itself. In that way each book denies that holy writ is unique, yet conversely each one affirms itself as an exercise in sainthood, inasmuch as sainthood consists in abandoning oneself to the mad [*insensée*] chance of sense. May there be, each time, in the scrolling of a volume, in the binding of a notebook, a burst of sense that shines and is eclipsed, and so on further and further, from book to book—*ta biblia* always echoing from one to the other, indefinitely and each time unique.

Can one not suppose, therefore, that the book is not solely, indeed not at all, a vehicle of or support for communication? It isn't a *medium*: it is immediately, itself, above all else, communication and commerce of itself with itself. Whoever really reads it enters into nothing less than that commerce with it. That is surely what constitutes its difference from the "lampoon" or "treatise." The latter documents transmit a message, whereas the book, if it can be said thus, communicates itself in person.

The book lays out its end in itself and comports itself as the envelope of an interiority. A unity and a uniqueness are implied in it—although it is no more a question of bringing them to the light of day than it is ever of showing the "soul" of a "person"—and that implication is all the more certain and demanding for its explanation being excluded or infinite (which comes down to the same thing). The open/closed book declares itself to be the topology of an inside that is constantly turned over into its outside: every book is a Moebius strip, in itself therefore finite and infinite, infinitely finite on all sides, opening a new margin on each page, each margin becoming wider, with a greater capacity for sense and secrecy.

The People of the Book

"Read me!" "Read me!"—that order or proposition occupies a major place in our culture, for we are those who, in one of our holy books, have designated ourselves *people of the Book*. "Read!" is what the prophet is ordered to do in that same book. "Take and read!" is, moreover, the command given to more than one character charged with divine mediation. "Read," or "Eat! swallow!" the book that is given to you. And we never stop (speaking of) devouring books, whether they taste bitter or sweet, of honey or poison.

What does the command to read signify? It is an ambiguous command, for it can as well enjoin us strictly to observe the law of the text as to interpret the sense of that text. However little attention one pays to it, one nevertheless quickly sees that those two injunctions are included neither equally nor symmetrically in the order that requires us to read. If one is to observe the law, one can only spell out the text, whereas, in order to interpret its sense, one has to decipher it. But in fact that difference extends much further or begins much earlier: law and text don't derive from the same reading, even when there exist a text and a book designated as those of the law. More precisely, as soon as the law offers itself to, or tends toward interpretation, it exceeds the strict register of the law. The law doesn't become a book, nor does its reading get produced as deciphering through its own means. The book presents the following difference: in the first place, it is outside of the law and answers to no jurisdiction other than that which it itself pronounces. Moreover, it can be said that there is no law in our tradition that does not exist before all reading (that is the sovereign aspect of the law, what makes it an exception to every other rule or principle and lays it down as truth), while at the same time remaining tributary to an explanation, an explicitation or unsealing (that is, therefore, its modalized or modulated textual aspect, which answers to the possibility of sense—albeit infinite—rather than truth). This double and essential postulation for the law in general exists as the principle of all our books of law, whether those of nomothetes, jurisconsults, or constituents, as well as those consecrated by our religions as "holy writ."

In general, the sacredness of the book consists in the fact that the book poses and imposes itself at one and the same time as a given, fully formed, integral and nonmodifiable entity, while also opening itself liberally to reading, which will never stop opening it wider and deeper, giving it a thousand senses or a thousand secrets, rewriting it, finally, in a thousand ways.

The commandment to read contains the principle of a necessary explanation of the immanent law of the book, which must also constitute the law of reading. That immanent law is none other than what I referred to earlier as "character." Reading consists in discerning the character proper to the book, and conversely, a book consists in modeling and modulating a character. That character can be indicated in many ways: for example, by the name of an author; or by a title combined with the mention of a genre; or still again, by means of a style, an accent [*frappe*], a manner of speaking, a procedure, or the "voice" I spoke of; or else by what can be called a force or charm, a power or intensity. But the synthetic or syncretic ideality of those potential designations is precisely what is called a *book*.

A book is an imprint—as I called it—and for that reason printing is not an accidental part of its history. The engraved and impressed characters now repeated in numerous copies on mobile supports, like those that preceded them, traced with a stylus and copied numerous times on skin, bark, or silk, comprise the imprint, the impregnation and pregnancy that the book is big and heavy with, whose volume, in fact, is nothing other than its womb and gravidity.

No birth results from it, however. The volume's fecundity develops as an interminable pregnancy. Never is there born the figure that would resemble the character's traits. The character tirelessly retains within itself the typeface [*type*], style [*poinçon*], or initial of its letter. That is because, in fact, type is nowhere fixed or given in advance. Unlike the stele, which has the law engraved upon it, no hieratic sovereignty erects or organizes the volume. Type is not stereotyped [*typé*], even less archetyped. The book, the great book, is the self-inscription of its character. And that inscription is mobile, labile, not fixed. Neither author, genre, style, nor energy allows itself to be determined by it: writing essentially displaces and deports every assigned recognition, every prescribed identification.

The character of the book—or rather, the character that the book *is*—consists only in its own tracing, and that tracing ends only by again taking up its own beginning. *Da capo* is the general register of the music of the book. Its reading is interminable, interminably recommenced, reprised, and renewed, for writing seeks nothing other than its own reprise, its becoming-refrain, its eternal return. Its characteristic is not a typology, hardly even a typography; it is only a "typic" in Kant's sense: the fragile analogue of a schema or movement, a sketch of the imagination for the creation of a monogram with mobile traits, intricate arabesques, an esoteric and ornamental calligraphy incessantly drawn toward uncertain borders, like some narrow mountain road whose tight curves run always close to the abyss. For ornament, in this case, is a matter of necessity, urgency, vigilance.

Reading comes down to driving on that road, never leaving it but never forgetting or warding off, either, the vertigo to which it is subject at every moment. "Interpreting" or "deciphering" the text doesn't mean returning the letter to its sense, but on the contrary, recomposing the cipher, all the figurings and encodings of the letter. It is not a matter of pulling meaning out of its envelope—for then it would immediately become good only for discarding—but rather of developing the enveloping as such: spreading it out, but by ceaselessly refolding upon itself whatever is deployed.

Interminable Reading

For that reason, painting has, during its history, given such a privileged place to the subjects of the book and reading. The man reading, the woman reading, the male or female bookworm, reciter, or reader [*la liseuse, la lectrice ou le lecteur*] are themselves also typic personages, for their type is that of the inexhaustible modalization and modulation of the book by reading, and of reading by the book. What is represented in a scene of reading? A gaze engrossed in a volume, a volume open for that gaze and opened by it, a mutual attraction and penetration. Perhaps the painter can find there a model or Idea for what he himself conceives of as gaze: not the distant vision of the object, but the thing's call to attention, the vigil before essence, the lookout for imminence.

What comes to the reader is a world, and that world comes to mingle with the plurality of worlds that he allows to inhabit him. Reading is a mêlée of worlds, a cosmogony in its genesis or its last agony, the potential, exponential, but always asymptotic characterization of a first and last congruence, taking place within the book but also between it and the cosmography of its time, whether that time be that of its writing or one of the times of its reading, one of those so numerous and varied times that occur once the book "endures the test of time," as we say. So it is that the reader of Plato, Montaigne, Milton or Lucan, James or Kafka, never finishes characterizing anew by means of their names and their titles—*Essays*, *Castle*, *Pupil*, *Pharsalus*, or *Paradise*—the polymorphous and protean schemes, the different (a)risings of storms or fevers, falls into torpor or sadness, precise or fleeting silhouettes, the whole heraldry of a galaxy that is each time put back into play, reformed, transformed.

It used to be said that the world itself was a great book: that didn't mean that its destiny was sealed in some kabbalistic scrawl; on the contrary, it showed that one had always, again and again, to manipulate its code, recombine its letters, and finally rewrite it. However full its history was of sound and fury—as is written in a book, and then, again, on the cover of another book—that sound

and fury are ours to concern ourselves with, and
it is their accents and traits, their graphology, in a
way, or their grammatology that we must recog-
nize.

The people of the Book that we are are people—
riffraff [*engeances*], generations, peoples, popula-
tions—to whom sense has not been given. Those
to whom sense was given, a consistent and com-
plete world, nature with its gods and powers, are
people of the Song or Stele, of the Hieroglyph
or Seal. For us, nothing has been given deriv-
ing from one or another of those figures. And the
book isn't a figure of that kind. Each such figure,
in fact, possesses at the outset a stature and tenor,
measure and authority. The book, by contrast, has
no form of assurance, nothing other than a buried,
perhaps undiscoverable character, not hidden but
rather dispersed, elusive, unrecognizable. Every
book dreams of becoming Hieroglyph or Song,
Stele or Seal. Each one wishes to represent itself
to itself as a rune, or else as a casket full of rare
coinage. But that desire is itself vague, errant, and
the book would cease being a book if it were to
change into a stone or a coffer.

To us no sense was given, instead, the commandment to read, not in order to find a sense that would have been hidden from us or refused us but in order to enter, in a quite different mode, into the space of an Idea that is precisely nothing other than the true and essential Form of the absence of given sense. Each book forms or formulates that Idea, each one characterizes and reiterates the effort to open once more its tracing—sinuous, uncertain, linear, but discontinuous, fragmentary, aleatory, multiple in itself as much as curled upon itself, in each case interminably so.

It nevertheless remains—or rather, emerges all the more strongly—that all books are compilations of hieroglyphs, collections of sacred characters, and assemblages of icons and emblems that comprise a cipher with inextricable permutations, which each reader in turn undertakes to recompose using the key to a different code and a reinvented mythology. Libraries and bookstores are the depots, reserves, and shopwindows of these coffers, whose locks must be forced before they are closed again with a new bolt and latch. Jean-François Champollion, who deciphered the Rosetta Stone, was the son of a book peddler. He taught himself to read, and he began his career working in a bookstore.

The Publication of the Unpublished

As a matter of principle, the book is illegible, and it calls for or commands reading in the name of that illegibility. Illegibility is not a question of what is too badly formed, crossed out, scribbled: the illegible is what remains closed in the opening of the book, what slips from page to page but remains caught, glued, stitched into the binding, or else laboriously jotted as marginalia that attempt to trip over the secret, that begin to write another book. What is illegible is not for reading at all, yet only by starting from it does something then offer itself to reading.

Of itself the book is untouched and sealed; it begins and ends in that sealing; it is always its own epitaph: *here lies an illegible one.* There is always a closed and inviolable book in the middle of every book that is opened, held apart between the hands that turn its pages, and whose every revolution, each turn from *recto* to *verso* begins again to fail to achieve its deciphering, to shed light on its sense.

For that reason every book, inasmuch as it is a book, is unpublished,[2] even though it repeats and replays individually, as each one does, the thousands of other books that are reflected in it like worlds in a monad. The book is unpublished [*inédit*], and it is that *inédit* that the publisher [*éditeur*] publishes. The *editor* (Latin)[3] is one who brings to the light of day, exposes to the outside, offers (*e-do*) to view and to knowledge. That doesn't, however, mean that once it is published the book is no longer unpublished; on the contrary, it remains that, and even becomes it more and more. It offers in full light of day, in full legibility, the insistent tracing of its illegibility.

"To edit" a book, in the English sense of the term, means to prepare a manuscript, to establish a definitive version of its text, lay out its presentation—the intricate work of preparation, reading, copyediting, mockup—watch over the bringing into evidence of its identity, its propriety, its closing also, and just as much, in consequence, its opening. More precisely still, it means opening, giving birth to, and handing over the closure of the book as such: its withdrawal, its secrecy, the illegibility in it that will never be divulged and that is destined for publication *as such*.

The publisher has already read that illegibility: he has read only that, as reader of the *idiogram* hidden in the text. The publisher is one who relates to the author rather than to the book, with him or her, or indeed that, which a movement of writing, a thinking, has carried and carried off toward the book without the author's knowing terribly much what that movement really is. The publisher accompanies that drift, gives it an outlet, captures it, and at the same time lets it go toward what doesn't come after but has already preceded: the "public," without which there would have been neither gesture of address nor tracing of writing.

One publishes for the public. "Publishing" doesn't mean divulging, nor is it a case of vulgarizing. It means blowing open the seals of an imaginary intimacy, of a privacy or exclusivity of the book. In the end, it means veritably to give to reading. Typography and page layout, printing, stitching or binding, packaging, window-, shelf-, or table-display are what make up entry into the commerce of thinking. Among those, exchange value, which is with good reason protected by law, doesn't reduce to a monetary equivalence without also signaling that it is a matter of a value in itself: to be worth something [*valoir*] is to count for someone other than oneself, and thinking counts essentially for the other, counts only for the other, by the other and in the other.

The bookstore occupies the site of that commerce: it is wholly occupied by the passage from one to another, from authors to readers, from publishers to authors and to readers, from one author to another, from booksellers to books and from books to readers, and further still, to those who don't read but who, nevertheless, from afar, without knowing it, are from one day to the next touched by words, by turns of phrase, by ways of saying and thinking that find themselves published and communicated here, find themselves sold and bought, suggested and chosen, confronted, affronted, ignored and forgotten also, each one enclosed and disclosed in its (il)legibility.

Formerly, the "bookseller" was everything in one: publisher, printer, and merchant, the private genie of author, work, or reader. That triple genius still haunts the book, fashioning it and exposing it, folding and unfolding it indefinitely upon itself and upon the world.

Book Open and Closed

That is why the book opens and closes, why its being a(s) book, its precarious and dazzling truth, resides in the internal conjunction and disjunction of that alternation: it opens and closes on the unique character whose tracing it contains. Hence it presents two aspects that are intimately dependent on each other: it is stitched and bound, it holds together as a body and forms a volume (that is the sense of the ancient *volumen*, the scroll that could be rolled around or unrolled from a core of wood or metal, ivory, reed, or bone), but at the same time it is discontinuous and a sheaf of leaves, the *codex* of stitched pages whose consistency only ever holds together by a thread. There was already *codex* in the *volumen*, just as there remains something of the latter in the former.

That is also why the book has two postures and two aspects: the volume that is put away and the volume that is open. On the one hand, the book noticed by the spine of its cover, its pages limited to the slice of their compact thinness; and, on the other hand, the open book with slightly raised pages, a finger sometimes slipped in ready to turn to the next one. These two books are both the same and not the same. As soon as one opens it, the first book loses the almost mute assurance of its compact consistency and its upright stance. It can no longer stand alone and no longer has, with its fellows, the appearance of an alignment, row, column, or flush stack of freshly cut bricks. It loses the superb and laconic stature of a cover that appears to tell it all, or better still, transmute it into a unique, homogeneous and nonanalyzable substance.

Substance, subordinate,[4] or subject, such was the closed book, that is to say, the book that is done, published, exposed, communicable, ready for selling or reading: cover, binding, title, author, publisher; there we have a subject, a particular agent. *La Chartreuse de Parme*, by Stendhal, Grenoble, Éditions Transalpines. The modes of stitching and binding, paper quality—tint, thickness, grain—also belong to that substantiality, as does the cover design, its colors, motifs, sometimes its images, the external as well as internal typography, the design and size of its fonts, its format, composition, running heads, its recto pages, correction of every sort of typo, so many discrete (and discreet) traits, whose totality derives from nothing other than an Idea or Character, a Typic Form that subsumes all the typographies, typologies, and characterologies implied in the publication of this volume. This subordinate, confected and fashioned by the publisher, mockup designer, copyeditor, and printer, refers each time, in one way or another, to the Idea of the Book itself, to some monumental Bible, some Koran with gilt-edged pages, some virgin Volume of Mallarmé, as well as to the sometimes severe, sometimes variegated look of the rows of volumes on bookshelves, collections, series, classifications by author, genre, period, to the whole taxonomy by means of which the Idea of a universal library or bookstore—and in the manner of the universe itself, every set that is finite and in infinite expansion—seeks to organize, if not to represent itself.

For it is on these shelves that the book is in fact exposed for the first time. On these shelves or display tables, these display stands or cabinets, in these windows as well, these bookcases, lofty fur-

nishings where one's gaze can just discern the titles on the top shelf. The library or bookstore—as
we know, they used to be the same thing—is nothing but the Idea of the book as exposed substance,
as subject that shows and presents itself. Here the
book pronounces its *ego sum*, *ego existo*, and, in
consequence, also its *cogito*. It is the very substance of itself, its whole nature consisting in its
relation to itself and in its obedience to its own
law, to the law of what is proper to it (its character,
idea, form, style, motion, and emotion . . .).

From that it follows that the bookstore is a place
where what is exhaled, and perhaps even exalt-
ed, in a very particular manner, is this regime
or climate of *monstration*, exhibition [*montre*] or
monstrance, the exposition and *ostention* that is in
force in general in what is called a store [*maga-
sin*], that is to say, a place for laying out for display or showing off the products of the ingenious
labor of invention [*labeur ingénieux*]. Each piece
of merchandise carries on and in itself—as its surface, aspect, sheen—the truly non-negotiable and
non-exchangeable price of the absolute value in it,
constituted by the subject of its production. That

"fetishistic" brilliance (to use Marx's word) is not always, or necessarily, perhaps never, or almost never exclusively, a deceptive luster, a mirage of "consumption" (however undeniable the importance and extent of that mirage, including in the domain of books): in principle it also retains something of the Idea that it issues from, whether that idea be that of the melon, herring, pen, armoire, or, indeed, book. However, in the bookstore the Idea intends precisely that the consumption of the merchandise—the devouring of the book—remain inseparable from a penetration into its intimacy, and that it be conducted in such a way that the gesture comes back to the gesture that gave birth to the book. As I have said, reading is what characterizes each time anew the character of the book. In a way, it reprints it. We could say that it republishes it: it rebinds [*relie*] it and rereads [*relit*] it each time afresh and involving new expense [*à nouveaux frais*], new stakes, new sense or lost sense.

That is what is required to open a book. There must be that moving and shaking of the play of opening and closing that is the only way that the book-subject can attain its real power: that is to say, by becoming the subject of a reading. Yet the opening doesn't take place, as one might think, only when whoever has acquired it has returned home, into a reading room or study, or only once the purchaser sets about cutting the folded pages of the book (to recall a scene that has today become very rare). The opening of the book begins once the publisher sends the book to the bookseller, whether that takes place by means of an automatic distribution process or by various kinds of information, publicity materials from the publisher, reviews in newspapers, specialized bulletins, or by rumor and contagion. Already indices are being provided, references, suggestions for reading, solicitations. Curiosity, desire, expectations are being awakened. Promises, invitations, exhortations are being noted. The bookseller is a transcendental reader: she provides her clients with the conditions of possibility for reading. A bookseller's customers are readers of reading at the same time as they are readers of the books they buy. The bookseller's reading doesn't only or simply consist in deciphering all the pages of every book; it is also a *lectio* as *electio*, a choice, selection, or gleaning of ideas from books that are proposed as a function of the Idea that bookseller has both of the book and of reading, both of readers and of publishers. In that sense, current usage doesn't call the bookseller a book merchant, putting aside what I just said about the commodity. Let's say, with less ambiguity, that the bookseller is one who delivers books [*un livreur de livres*]: he brings them and exposes them, giving them the vantage from which to play their role as subjects.

But at the same time, immediately, the bookseller opens them a second time. In the same way that they have been opened for him or by him in the context of a choice about display, highlighting, inviting, so has he by that very process set in train their opening by the fingers of those visiting the store. The election and presentation, the whole argumentative, rhetorical, and encyclopedic apparatus of which the bookstore is the material machine in action, and of which booksellers are the inventive soul, all of that leads to the gesture made by a future reader.

The Scents of the Bookstore

Librarium: *box or case for the storage of* volumina.
Librarius: *educated slave charged with the task of
reading out loud or copying books and maintaining the
library in good order.*

Once opened, the book reveals how insubstan-
tial it is. The substance, subordinate, or subject
doesn't really disappear, but rather is unfolded and
disassembled, although continuing to hold together thanks to glue or sewing, thanks to the grasp
of the book's spine. As for the belly, the belly or
chest is parted, allowing itself to be observed between its pages, page by page or leaf by leaf, from
leaf to leaf by chance, just to see. That is called
leafing through. The reader in a bookstore doesn't
read, or reads very little, but he leafs through, in-
spects by groping his way, almost in the dark. He
doesn't devour, but tastes, inhales, sniffs, or licks
the substance.

The bookstore is a perfumery, rotisserie, patis-
serie: a dispensary of scents and flavors through
which something like a fragrance or bouquet of

the book is divined, presumed, sensed. It is where one gives oneself or finds an idea of the book's Idea, a sketch, an allusion, a suggestion. Perhaps it speaks of what one was looking for, what one was hoping for. Perhaps it keeps the promise made by its title (*Lost Time*, *Being and Nothingness*, *Captain Fracasse*) or by the name of its author (Diderot, Joachim de Flore, Ernest Hemingway, Jane Austen) or again by the name of its publisher or series—(Galican, Calmy-Cohen, Enseignes, Portulans, le Typographe). Perhaps, better still, it keeps the discreet promise of the unknown, the unexpected—*The Intruder*, *On Peas with Bacon*, *Story of a Journey through a Great Bookstore*—or else, perhaps, devoid of all promise and avoiding thereby the risk of breaking any, it simply confirms its seriousness, its competence—*The Real Story of My Life*, *The Origin of Geomancy*, *Tristan and Isis*.

The bookstore opens to the reader the general space of all kinds of opening, furtive glance, brief shedding of light or illumination, drilling, prospecting, sifting, fine-tooth combing, sampling, or summary. It is always a matter of unbinding the tie that holds the volume together and of letting it breathe, puff for a second, a matter also of having it lose its sufficiency and consistency enough so that it can be found only in the zealousness or nonchalance of the fingers that turn its pages.

But the glance also leafs through the shelves and tables, settling here and there, jumping from color to format, guided by silhouettes, images, various signals. It lets itself be seduced, solicited, charmed. It judges the thicknesses, skims through the back cover blurbs, or, where they still exist, the flysheets [*prière d'insérer*]. The glance is what is being asked to "pray insert" into the book some of its desire, its curiosity, the imagination that is always at its back, keeping it waiting for worlds, narratives, contentment, knowledge.

Even touching books communicates to the reader particular impressions: the weight, grain, or suppleness through which one thinks one can discern the inflections of a voice or else the fluctuations of a heart.

In all these declensions and decompositions of the book the uncertain contour of its Idea is vibrating: no longer substance but sense in instance, no longer subject but malleable, ductile, fluid, and sometimes gaseous thing, volatile, disseminated into the air and mingling with the aerosols of all other books. The Idea itself evaporates and separates from its original orbit; it begins to be redrawn, to come undone, to loosen its moorings on the way to tracing other volutes, other sketchings and contours that will be the features of inventive, dreamy, inquisitive, or negligent readings, at the whim of each reader but also according to what each book is able to do with that reader, or against her, unknown to her or before her eyes.

For, in the end, the Idea of the book will always, from its very first conception, have been the Idea of its reading and, through that reading, the Idea of another book, of another writing that continues on from the first. Not necessarily the writing of another book, but at the very least the writing of another tracing of thinking, another curve, volute, or meander of representation, of meditation, imitation, or creation. The Idea of the book is the Idea that there is no end to this very Idea, and that it contains nothing less than its own proliferation, its multiplication, its dispersion, and always, at some moment and in some respect or another, there is the silent or eloquent advice from the book that is an invitation to throw it away, to abandon it. In fact reading does not lead to more reading, but to everything else, to what is sometimes called action and sometimes experience, where we rub up against the illegible real.

All the same, it is only by always reading anew that one can discard books one by one. Throw them not on the pyre or into oblivion, but launch them further and more profoundly into what should, with just cause, be called the bookstore of the soul, the free space of a devouring of and by the pure Idea, the labyrinth of books that are read, jotted on, forgotten, and dust-covered, the books learned and forgotten by heart, the creasing of the edges of pages whose image always comes back because they contain certain precious words.

The Commerce of Thinking

But the book that is thrown into the depths of such a bookstore, magazine of traces, imprints and reminiscences—the bookstore whose other, the shop on the street, is in sum nothing but an inverted reflection, such as appears where a palace is surrounded by large pools of water—the book so expedited into memory and hackneyed repetition, into whispered recitation, also finds in that subterranean recollection the expansiveness and lightness of a flight into free air.

For the book always and only goes from Idea to Idea, and its opening, its enlivened and loosened pages, followed from right to left and from top to bottom, or in the opposite directions and following every possible combination, its patient and meticulous readings as well as its greedy and hurried ones, its studies, commentaries, glosses, analyses, plagiarisms and parodies, only spread ever more widely, ever more impalpably, the substance of its Idea, which ends up losing itself by finding itself metamorphosed, metempsychosed, or metaphorized into other books, into innumerable volumes, booklets, lampoons, essays, pamphlets, opuscules become volumes themselves once more, folios, quartos, octavos, into indefinitely multiplied issues that disperse into the air the dust of sense and ashes of the Idea, an Idea in ashes not for having been put on the pyre (the smoke of auto-da-fés, whose name is so repugnant, represents the exact opposite of the book, and piling up a bonfire is an exact figure of the demolition of the bookstore and its shelves), but for having been liberally scattered into the vast cosmos through which shines the star shower of the Idea. A book is a meteor that breaks up into thousands of meteorites whose random courses provoke collisions, strokes of genius, sudden crystallizations of new books, unpublished tracings of characters, enlarged, revised, and corrected editions, an immense interstellar circulation.

A book always dreams of becoming an aerolith in flames, a comet whose flaming mane consumes the Idea into the dust of glory and the experience of the infinite. The bookstore opens this free air of experience, of the risk and chance of a glimpse at what cannot be seen, what in the Idea exceeds every form and every character. The bookstore always keeps deep within itself something of the hawker of books, that strapping fellow loaded down with little *duodecimos* and *sextodecimos*, booklets falling out of his sack and slipped into his coattails or hat, adept not only at selling them but at advertising them too, and, if necessary, reciting them by heart from beginning to end—*Manon Lescaut*, *Young Werther*, or *Sheherazade*—a nomad shopkeeper and storyteller, walking bard, strolling door-to-door merchant [*marchand marcheur et démarcheur*] of cheap editions, bookstore in sunshine and rain of the fields and strand and open road. A bookstore is always found on the edge of a grand avenue that leads nowhere but from book to book, delivered over to itself and following the tracks of its idea, word for word indefinitely reprinted, a grand avenue along which this emotional and subtle commerce of thinking never ceases, for in it is resumed and consumed the pure and always novel form of what we call the book.

The Matter of Books

Perhaps what we name thus is only the name and the idea, its ideal, its ideality, the pure *scription* of an available truth sealed with a clasp of ink and paper. Perhaps there is never anywhere, all through its deliveries, a single book. Perhaps the bookish always stifles writing, or perhaps writings murder voices. Perhaps there are only reports and studies, accounts and compilations, fantasy and sycophancy. It remains nevertheless that the commerce of our thoughts, by means of which we are kept together, however loosely or badly that be, relies on the circulation of a currency whose incalculable unit is named "book."

It is not the unit of a sense, but of a matter that carries the promise of thinking. By means of a peculiar relation to *liber*, *Baum* and *Buch* in German, *book* in English, the tree and the book have the same root, derived from engraved wood. Wax, wood, papyrus, parchment, vellum, luminous screen—what is always involved is sensitive matter, a supple and ductile thickness that offers self for cutting or imprinting, that is capable of accepting the mark and retaining the trace without taking away from it its transitory character, its potential effacement: a collection or gathering [*recueil*], a reverent contemplation [*recueillement*], and a fugitiveness, a forgetting, a fragility.

Books are heavy and light, they come one after the other, they substitute one for another even as they remain immobilized on solemn library shelves. They are simply books [*bouquins*] and illegible mumbo jumbo as much as first editions and incunabula. They are easily set alight, but difficult to consume. They are the matter of our thinking, serious yet elusive, available yet secret, obstinately shared among us as the promise of nothing other than this commerce itself.

Electronic Supplement, Binary
Reprise, Digital Counterpoint

Liber: membrane occurring between bark and wood, between *cortex* and *lignum*, between exposed thought and knotty intimacy, interface between outside and inside, itself neither outside nor inside, turned toward one as toward the other, turning one toward the other, turning one back over into the other. Although the book can become—digitized, immaterialized and virtualized as well as bound in leather and gilt-edged—however slim it may become, it can be produced only by remaining "for this reader pure block—transparent," through which we gain access to nothing other than ourselves, some to others but in each to hieroglyphics.

Pure block—transparent reader screen before the screen face reflecting white vibrating glimmer within which appear and disappear the signs of the virtual book: the same, the

same; signs, but caught in this other-world brilliance, oth-
erworldliness that removes them from reading and pre-
sents them for capture . . .

No book ever flows from a source: one doesn't
write a book as one writes a letter, memoir, or lampoon (*libelle*, "little book"). One projects, rather, an enterprise that thinks of itself, each time,
as having no example and no imitator. One envisages delivering [*livrer*], or delivering oneself, as
a thought that is perfect in itself and sufficient to
itself, never a simple means of communication,
representation, or imagination. A book is born
in agitation and anxiety, in the fermentation of a
form in search of itself, in search of a deployment
and appeasement for its impatience.

On screen impatience grows at the speed of digital opera-
tions, captures, erasures, cut-and-pastes, transfers, trans-
formations—fonts, sizes, colors, shadings, formats, indents,
bullets, paragraphs—a pixelated fever takes over all these
simultaneously open windows within which why not write
ten simultaneous texts or a single one composed of pieces
that fly off in all directions?

Can one not suppose, therefore, that the book is not solely, indeed not at all, a vehicle of or support for communication? It isn't a *medium*: it is immediately, itself, above all else, communication and commerce of itself with itself. Whoever really reads it enters into nothing less than that commerce with it.

The screen neither, not a medium, nor a message either, but a milky way, exactly, luminous sister of white streams no longer those of Canaan but of a subtle and ductile electricity propagating an uninterrupted excitement in a text that perhaps in the end says only that, that it is excited in favor of its own propagation

A book is an imprint—as I called it—and for that reason printing is not an accidental part of its history. The engraved and impressed characters now repeated in numerous copies on mobile supports, like those that preceded them, traced with a stylus and copied numerous times on skin, bark, or silk, comprise the imprint, the impregnation and pregnancy that the book is big and heavy with, whose volume, in fact, is nothing other than its womb and gravidity.

Imprint nevertheless always the character appearing on the screen carried along at the whim the rhythm the speed of fingers on the keyboard like a piano a harpsichord an organ a harmonium or even xylophone or vibraphone in fact electronic music, yes, text becoming more musical more strident more sharp more penetrating more rapidly fleeing dissipating into the air text evaporating on the surface of the screen splattered by keystrokes

For that reason, painting has, during its history, given such a privileged place to the subjects of the book and reading. The man reading, the woman reading, the male or female bookworm, reciter, or reader [*la liseuse, la lectrice ou le lecteur*] are themselves also typic personages, for their type is that of the inexhaustible modalization and modulation of the book by reading, and of reading by the book. What is represented in a scene of reading? A gaze engrossed in a volume, a volume open for that gaze and opened by it, a mutual attraction and penetration.

She is reading what is she reading? We won't know and she is reading what isn't legible for us but she is reading it or perhaps she is who knows pretending to read just to offer herself to our gaze.

We can easily see that she likes us to look at her and think we can decipher not her book but her soul.

It used to be said that the world itself was a great book: that didn't mean that its destiny was sealed in some kabbalistic scrawl; on the contrary, it showed that one had always, again and again, to manipulate its code, recombine its letters, and finally rewrite it.

Every book dreams of becoming Hieroglyph or Song, Stele or Seal. Each one wishes to represent itself to itself as a rune, or else as a casket full of rare coinage. But that desire is itself vague, errant, and the book would cease being a book if it were to change into a stone or a coffer.

If it changes into a screen, no longer block, stone, or box, but plasma, pane, transparent, cellophane, diaphany, epiphany, fireflies, glowworms of a new prosody

Substance, subordinate, or subject, such was the

closed book, that is to say, the book that is done, published, exposed, communicable, ready for selling or reading: cover, binding, title, author, publisher; there we have a subject, a particular agent. *La Chartreuse de Parme*, by Stendhal, Grenoble, Éditions Transalpines. The modes of stitching and binding, paper quality—tint, thickness, grain—also belong to that substantiality, as does the cover design, its colors, motifs, sometimes its images, the external as well as internal typography, the design and size of its fonts, its format, composition, running heads, its recto pages, correction of every sort of typo, so many discrete (and discreet) traits, whose totality derives from nothing other than an Idea or Character, a Typic Form that subsumes all the typographies, typologies, and characterologies implied in the publication of this volume. This subordinate, confected and fashioned by the publisher, mockup designer, copyeditor, and printer, refers each time, in one way or another, to the Idea of the Book itself, to some monumental Bible, some Koran with gilt-edged pages, some virgin Volume of Mallarmé, as well as to the sometimes severe, sometimes variegated look of the rows of volumes on bookshelves, collections, series, classifications by author, genre, period, to the whole taxonomy by means of which the Idea of a universal library or bookstore—and in the manner of the universe itself, every set that is finite and in infinite expansion—seeks to organize, if not to represent itself.

Indefinite expansion and in every sense, in all directions of the internal invisible proliferation of virtual pages that the screen swallows and bounces back, digests and regurgitates at will, and where do they go, lying low, compressed, vaporized, reduced to a gaseous state a luminous state in order to spring back out of storage shining and ready for printing again for Gutenberg returns as a rapid laser jet burst of ink printer blocks of wood transmuted into ink cartridges or black powder but what always comes back is pressure, stamping, inking, how to do without ink shining in the middle of this lucid sky?

All the same, it is only by always reading anew that one can discard books one by one. Throw them not on the pyre or into oblivion, but launch them further and more profoundly into what should, with just cause, be called the bookstore of the soul, the free space of a devouring of and by the pure Idea, the labyrinth of books that are read, jotted on, forgotten, and dust-covered, the books learned and forgotten by heart, the creasing of the edges of pages whose image always comes back because they contain certain precious words.

Some pricey words: screen, icon, capture, rush, command, mouse, tabulation, pad, control, file, page, menu, disk . . .

It is not the unit of a sense, but of a matter that carries the promise of thinking. By means of a peculiar relation to *liber*, *Baum* and *Buch* in German, *book* in English, the tree and the book have the same root, derived from engraved wood. Wax, wood, papyrus, parchment, vellum, luminous screen—what is always involved is sensitive matter, a supple and ductile thickness that offers itself for cutting or imprinting, that is capable of accepting the mark and retaining the trace without taking away from it its transitory character, its potential effacement: a collection or gathering [*recueil*], a reverent contemplation [*recueillement*], and a fugitiveness, a forgetting, a fragility.

Books are heavy and light, they come one after the other, they substitute one for another even as they remain immobilized on solemn library shelves. They are simply books [*bouquins*] and illegible mumbo jumbo as much as first editions and incunabula. They are easily set alight, but difficult to consume. They are the matter of our thinking, serious yet elusive, available yet secret, obstinately shared among us as the promise of nothing other than this commerce itself.

Without either volumen or codex or turned pages but on-screen or saved pages, bursting to the surface of water of ice of cottonwool of down of virtual swans renewing or drowning out this uninterrupted commerce nothing other than us ourselves changing always more into us others priceless commerce exchanging with each other or all of us changing into milky crystal swarm of insect pixels abandoned to their gnat dance in this moonbeam, finally abandoned and perhaps even delivered from every book and every sign and . . . .

$(\cdots)^5$

Notes

Translator's Preface: Thinking Singular Plural

1. Jean-Luc Nancy, *Being Singular Plural*, trans. Robert D.
   Richardson and Anne E. O'Byrne (Stanford: Stanford
   University Press, 2000), 154, 147, 148; trans. modified.
2. Ibid., 156.

On the Commerce of Thinking

1. Stéphane Mallarmé, *Notes en vue du Livre,"* in *Œuvres
   complètes* (Paris: Gallimard, 1998), 1:970: "et le livre est
   pour ce lecteur bloc pur-transparent."
2. *Inédit*, also "novel," "original."—TRANS.
3. The word is masculine, as are several others (printer
   [*imprimeur*] in absolute usage, corrector [*correcteur*] in
   generic usage), but we know to what extent these
   professions are peopled by women and how much the
   book, in general, owes to women. Moreover, the reader
   [*lecteur*] is not exactly a generic noun, for it is clear,
   and not by chance, that female readers [*lectrice, liseuse*]
   are special figures, in whom reading is identified with

58

a special intensity. The noun "bookseller [*libraire*]," for its part, has the advantage of being bisexed, in the manner of each of us.

4. Nancy's word here and elsewhere is *suppôt*, which is rare and used almost exclusively for a "person" in the sense of "underling" or "henchman," as in *un suppôt de Satan*. Pierre Klossowski often used the word in the context of his rewriting of subjectivity. It is derived from Latin *supponere*, "to place under," and so echoes with, and between, "substance" ("standing under," usually understood in terms of the materiality of an object) and "subject" ("thrown under," the traditional philosophical term relating to persons).—TRANS.

5. This text translates Jean-Luc Nancy, "Supplément électronique, reprise numérique, contrepoint digital," which appeared in Jean-Noël Blanc, ed., *363000 Signes, la chaîne graphique* (Saint-Etienne: Éditions des Cahiers intempestifs, 2006). *Numérique* in Nancy's title is equivalent to English "digital" in high-technology parlance; by "binary," I seek to evoke computer technology and also retain the semantic link to "numerical."—TRANS.